HARRIET *Tubman*

SPIRIT
of America®

HARRIET *Tubman*

ABOLITIONIST AND UNDERGROUND RAILROAD CONDUCTOR

By Cynthia Klingel

*Content Adviser: The Reverend Paul G. Carter, Director,
The Harriet Tubman Home, Auburn, New York*

The Child's World®
Chanhassen, Minnesota

7

HARRIET *Tubman*

Published in the United States of America by The Child's World®
PO Box 326 • Chanhassen, MN 55317-0326 • 800-599-READ • www.childsworld.com

Acknowledgments
The Child's World®: Mary Berendes, Publishing Director

Editorial Directions, Inc.: E. Russell Primm, Editorial Director; Pam Rosenberg, Line Editor; Elizabeth K. Martin, Assistant Editor; Olivia Nellums, Editorial Assistant; Susan Hindman, Copy Editor; Susan Ashley, Halley Gatenby, Proofreaders; Jean Cotterell, Kevin Cunningham, Peter Garnham, Fact Checkers; Tim Griffin/IndexServ, Indexer; Dawn Friedman, Photo Researcher; Linda S. Koutris, Photo Selector

Photo
Cover: Hulton Archive/Getty Images; Dennis Reavis, The Daily Journal/AP/Wide World Photos: 13; Courtesy of National Parks Service/AP/Wide World Photos: 17; photographer Jack Kidd, Coburn Design, and Cayuga County (NY) Office of Tourism: 23, 28; Corbis: 6, 11, 18, 22, 25; Bettmann/Corbis: 7 bottom, 8, 12, 15, 16, 20, 21, 26; Hulton Archive/Getty Images: 2, 9, 10, 14, 19, 27; Library of Congress, 7 top..

Library of Congress Cataloging-in-Publication Data
Klingel, Cynthia Fitterer.
  Harriet Tubman : abolitionist and Underground Railroad conductor / by Cynthia Klingel.
     p. cm. — (Our people)
"Spirit of America."
Summary: Provides a brief introduction to Harriet Tubman, her accomplishments, and her impact on American history. Includes bibliographical references (p.) and index.
  ISBN 1-59296-004-9 (lib. bdg. : alk. paper)
1. Tubman, Harriet, 1820?–1913—Juvenile literature. 2. Slaves—United States—Biography—Juvenile literature.
3. African American women—Biography—Juvenile literature. 4. Underground railroad—Juvenile literature.
[1. Tubman, Harriet, 1820?–1913. 2. Slaves. 3. African Americans—Biography. 4. Women—Biography. 5. Underground railroad.] I. Title. II. Series.
  E444.T82K558 2003
  973.7'115—dc21   2003004163

12   18   27

Contents

A Hard Life

HARRIET TUBMAN IS ONE OF THE MOST FAMOUS women in American history. She is responsible for helping hundreds of slaves escape to freedom during the 1800s. Today, more than 180 years after her birth, we still celebrate her for her **courage** and strength.

Harriet Tubman was born sometime around 1820. It is almost impossible to know for sure because records of slaves' births and deaths were not always kept. She was named Araminta at birth. Later, she took the name Harriet, after her mother. Her parents were Benjamin Ross and Harriet Greene. They were slaves owned by Master

Edward Brodas. He owned a large **plantation** near Cambridge, Maryland, where they and his other slaves worked.

Harriet's childhood was very hard. When she was six years old, she was taken from her parents and given to a nearby family. She had to work inside all day. She was **miserable.** Then she became sick. She was returned to Master Brodas.

She was happy to be back on the plantation with her parents. Her mother and father took care of her, and Master Brodas let her stay there for a while. Then, he rented her to another family. She was only seven years old.

For the new family, she had to do housework and care for the baby during the nights. Harriet was whipped if she didn't do the housework well or if the baby cried during the night. She was very

Harriet Tubman lived in slave quarters like these as a young child.

Young slave children were often sent to work in the homes of plantation owners. They had to do whatever the plantation owner's family—even the children—told them to do.

unhappy there. Finally, she was sent back to Master Brodas. He put her to work in the fields.

Working in the fields was hard physical work. She was working with many of the men. She tried hard to keep up with them. She heard them telling stories of slaves trying to run away to freedom. The stories of slave catchers with dogs were frightening. But like many of the others, Harriet dreamed about being free. She was not afraid.

Harriet was not willing to be treated the way other slaves were. She did not pretend to be nice to her master or his family. One day, when Harriet was about 12 or 13 years old, she was told by an **overseer** to help stop a slave who was attempting to escape. She refused. The overseer was very angry. He picked up a heavy iron

Working in plantation fields was hard, tiring work.

weight and threw it at the escaping slave. It missed him and hit Harriet in the head.

Harriet was badly injured. She was **unconscious** for days and almost died. Her mother and father cared for her while she was unconscious. During this time, Master Brodas tried to sell her. But no one would buy a slave who was so sick. Even when she began to recover, she was very weak from being unconscious for so long. Slowly she grew stronger. But she would fall asleep instantly, at any time. She had no control over these sleeping spells. They were a result of her head injury and continued for the rest of her life.

Overseers watched over the slaves working in the fields and often treated the slaves badly.

Interesting Fact

▸ Some historians believe Harriet Tubman could have been born any time between 1816 and 1823.

9

IN THE EARLY 1600S, THE ENGLISH BEGAN TO SETTLE IN NORTH AMERICA. SOME of the earliest colonists settled in Virginia. Over time, tobacco became one of the most valuable crops grown in Virginia. Tobacco was grown on large farms called plantations. Eventually, the plantation system of farming spread, especially in the southern regions of what would become the United States of America.

Other crops grown on plantations were cotton, sugar cane, and rice. All of these crops require a lot of work to grow and harvest. Plantation owners were in need of a cheap supply of labor. To fill the need for workers, many men and women came to America as **indentured servants.** Convicts sent from Great

Britain to serve out their terms by working on plantations were another source of cheap labor. These sources did not supply enough people to cover the huge needs of the plantation owners. Eventually, they began to purchase slaves to work their fields.

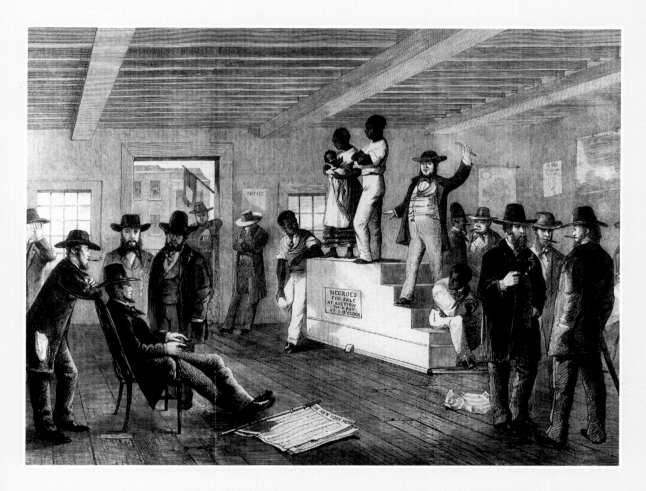

The economy of the southern United States was based on farming. Slavery became a very important part of the way of life in southern states. Farms in the North tended to be smaller than those in the South. Also, through the years, industries other than farming began to be much more profitable in the northern states. Eventually, slavery died out in the northern United States. This difference between the northern and southern states would eventually lead to the Civil War.

Chapter TWO

Journey toward Freedom

WHEN HARRIET RECOVERED, SHE WENT BACK to working in the fields. Although she was only 4 feet 11 inches (150 centimeters) tall, she was as strong as any man. When she was about 14, Master Brodas died. Her new master was John Stewart. He told her to work alongside her father cutting down trees.

Harriet and her father had many talks while they worked. Harriet told her father about her dream to be free. He could see that she was determined. Through the years he taught her about the woods. He taught her

Sometimes slave children worked in the fields with their parents.

This home in Wilmington, Illinois, was a station on the Underground Railroad.

how to tell directions, what plants to eat, how to catch small animals, and how to hide in the woods. She would need to know all of this if she wanted to successfully escape.

In 1844, when Harriet was about 24 years old, she married John Tubman. John was a free black man. Even though he was free, it was hard for him to get a job. No one wanted to hire and pay a black man. John lived with Harriet on the plantation.

Harriet Tubman still dreamed of being free. She heard stories of slaves traveling the Underground Railroad to freedom. She found out that this was not a real railroad and it wasn't really underground. It was many houses and places where white and black

13

Fugitive slaves often had to cross rivers on their way to freedom.

people helped slaves travel from the plantations where they lived to Pennsylvania. In Pennsylvania, slaves were free. The people who helped slaves along the railroad were called conductors. Everything about the Underground Railroad was a secret and very mysterious.

One day in 1849, Tubman learned how to escape on the Underground Railroad. She got this information just in time. She had found out that Master Stewart was planning to send her far south to be sold. During the night, she made her escape. No one knew she was leaving. She had not told her mother, father, or John. She followed the directions she had been given. She went north to the Choptank River. Then she followed the river for many miles to the town of Camden, Delaware. From there, she went to Wilmington, Delaware. This trip took many days. She had to travel by night and hide from the slave catchers. She was very afraid she would have one of her sleeping

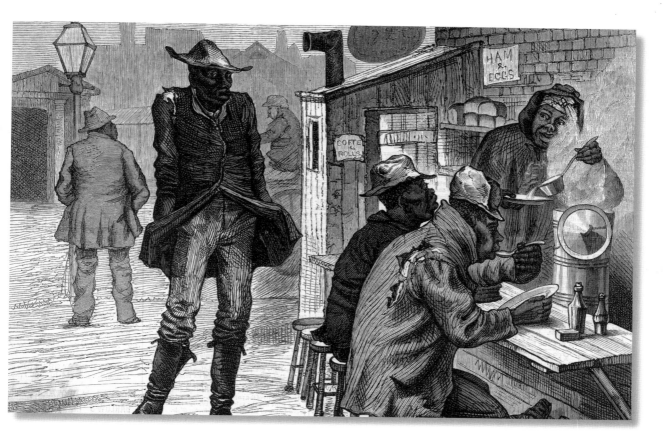

spells and would be found. Finally, she arrived in Philadelphia, Pennsylvania. She was free! It is recorded that she said, "When I found I had crossed that line, I looked at my hands to see if I was the same person."

Tubman settled in Philadelphia and began working as a cook. She met William Still, the Philadelphia stationmaster on the Railroad. He taught her many things about how the Railroad worked. She couldn't forget the family she had left. She was determined to help them escape to freedom.

Harriet Tubman settled in Philadelphia, Pennsylvania, and worked as a cook.

15

THE UNDERGROUND RAILROAD WAS A SECRET NETWORK OF ESCAPE routes. Most of these routes led from the South to northern free states and then to Canada. A few routes went to Mexico and the countries of the Caribbean. The Railroad was used most between the late 1700s and 1865. That was a period when many white people did not agree with slavery. They assisted the slaves as they escaped.

"Conductors" used many different strategies to help the slaves. Many white and black people helped. They often drove wagons with the escapees hiding underneath grain and vegetables. Sometimes the wagons had false bottoms, so although the wagon looked empty, several people might actually be hiding underneath. The conductors often

used disguises, and other people helped get them the necessary supplies. Experts think thousands of black slaves found freedom through the Underground Railroad. But no one is sure exactly how many. Most conductors and stationmasters, like Lewis Hayden (left), did not record names or details of the people who escaped. The conductors were very careful not to keep information that could be used to find their "passengers."

The need for the Underground Railroad ended in December 1865. The 13th Amendment to the Constitution of the United States was signed. It gave freedom to every person in the United States, and slavery became illegal.

Chapter THREE

A Leader of Her People

African-American slaves escaping on the Underground Railroad often traveled at night to avoid being caught.

IN 1850, HARRIET TUBMAN RETURNED TO Maryland through the Underground Railroad to help her family. First, she brought her sister and her sister's family to freedom. Then she returned for her brothers and their families. She went back a third time to rescue her husband. But when she got there, she learned that he had married another woman. So Tubman gathered others and guided them to safety. By now, the trip had gotten longer. Pennsylvania was no longer safe for

William Still, a friend of Tubman's, published The Underground Railroad *in 1871.*

runaway slaves. Tubman had to lead them all the way to Canada.

Harriet Tubman quickly became a well-known conductor on the Underground Railroad. She made a total of 19 trips and rescued more than 300 slaves between 1851 and 1860. The white plantation owners offered a $40,000 reward for her **capture**. This was a fortune at that time.

Tubman was willing to do whatever it took to rescue slaves, even though she suffered great hardship. William Still,

Tubman's friend in Philadelphia, published *The Underground Railroad* in 1871. In it is part of a letter he received from another stationmaster, Thomas Garret. It said, "We made arrangements last night and sent away Harriet Tubman, with six men and one woman . . . to be forwarded across the country to the city. Harriet, and one of the men, had worn the shoes off their feet, and I gave them two dollars to help fit them out and directed a carriage to be hired at my expense, to take them out."

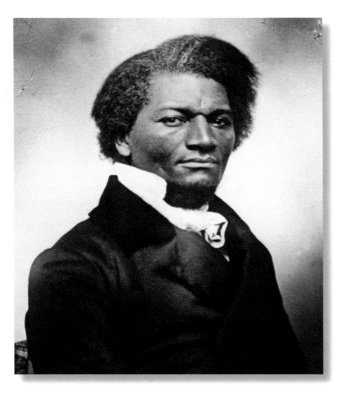

Frederick Douglass was a famous African-American abolitionist.

Another famous black American, Frederick Douglass, knew Tubman. He once said that except for a man named John Brown, there was no one who had willingly **encountered** more **perils** and hardships to serve black slaves than Harriet Tubman.

Tubman was nicknamed Moses by her people. They named her after the prophet Moses who led the children of Israel out of

Egypt into the Promised Land. Tubman was proud of her success. She gladly declared that she had never run her train off the track, and she had never lost a passenger. Not one slave was captured or killed while escaping with Harriet. She was a very religious woman who believed that she was successful because God sent her where she should go. She believed God helped her to know what to do when there was trouble.

There are many reasons why Harriet Tubman was so successful. She was smart and made excellent decisions. She was a master at disguising herself. She was also a strong leader.

Harriet Tubman (far left) is pictured here with some of the former slaves she helped.

Interesting Fact

▶ John Brown, a famous white man, once said that Harriet Tubman was one of the bravest persons in America. He referred to her as "General Tubman."

▶ Some experts think there were 3,000 "conductors" on the Underground Railroad. They also think that more than 100,000 slaves escaped this way.

William Seward was a U.S. senator who helped Tubman purchase a home in Auburn, New York.

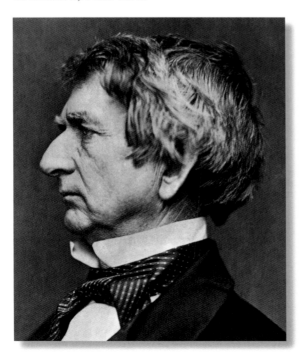

She did not allow her passengers to be afraid or weak. Tubman knew that if any of the passengers got scared and returned to their masters, the rest of the group would be in great danger. She could not let any of her secrets be shared, so she carried a gun. If any of the slaves acted like they were going to turn back, she would point her gun at them and threaten to shoot them if they didn't continue with her on the trip.

Tubman often traveled the road between Syracuse and Rochester, New York. Many people along this route helped her and the people she was leading. One couple on the route was William and Frances Seward. William Seward was a U.S. senator and former New York state governor. He and his wife lived in the town of Auburn. When Tubman helped her niece escape, the young woman went to live with the Sewards. It was the Sewards who, in 1859, helped Tubman to purchase the house where she lived with her parents.

TODAY, VISITORS CAN WALK THROUGH HARRIET TUBMAN'S HOME IN AUBURN, New York. The Harriet Tubman Home is a collection of four buildings. They are located on 32 acres (13 hectares) of land. Tubman lived in two of the buildings. The site is now owned by the African Methodist Episcopal (AME) Zion Church and operated by The Harriet Tubman Home, Inc.

Tubman purchased the first home and 7 acres (3 ha) of land with the help of her friend, U.S. senator William H. Seward. At that time, it was illegal to sell property to African-Americans. Tubman brought her parents to this home to live. After she married Nelson Davis in 1869, they lived in the wooden house on the property. After a fire, this house was rebuilt with bricks.

In 1896, Tubman bought an additional 25 acres (10 ha). She wanted to build a home for needy black people on the land but couldn't raise enough money. In 1903, she **deeded** the land to the AME Zion Church. The Harriet Tubman Home was opened in 1908. Tubman cared for old and needy people who lived in the home until shortly before her death. The Harriet Tubman Home was closed a few years after Tubman's death.

The Harriet Tubman Home building was vacant from 1928 until 1944. That was the year the city ordered it to be torn down. A fund drive raised $30,000 to restore the home and save it from demolition. In 1953, the newly restored home was dedicated to the memory of Harriet Tubman.

The Fight Continues

THE PEOPLE OF THE UNITED STATES COULD not agree about whether slavery should be allowed. Many people in the northern states were against slavery. Many leaders in the southern states were ready to fight for their right to own slaves. The southern states declared that they were no longer part of the United States. They formed their own country called the Confederate States of America.

In 1861, the Civil War broke out. Harriet Tubman joined the war effort. She worked as a nurse and took care of wounded **Union** soldiers at a U.S. Army hospital. Later, she was asked to organize secret troops among the slaves in the area. She became a spy and a scout. Her years of traveling the Underground Railroad made her very good

at this. She knew the countryside very well, and she knew how to travel without being seen or caught.

On June 2, 1863, Tubman led a group of 300 black soldiers up the Combahee River to raid a Confederate camp. They freed 800 slaves and destroyed all the supplies. This was a big victory for the Union Army. Tubman was a hero. Articles about her were published in many of the newspapers.

Many African-Americans fought for the Union during the Civil War.

In her later years,
Harriet Tubman became
active in the women's
rights movement.

Interesting Fact

▶ Today, there is a
name for the strange
sleeping spells that
Harriet had through-
out her life. It is
called narcolepsy.

In 1865, the Civil War ended. Slavery
was outlawed in the United States. Harriet
Tubman was exhausted. She returned to her
home in Auburn, New York. By now,
Tubman was in her early 40s.

Although the black slaves were now free,
Tubman saw that many African-American
people were not successful. They did not lead
better lives. They still could not read or write.
It was hard to get a decent job. Harriet
Tubman wanted to help.

In 1869, Tubman married Nelson Davis. Tubman had met Davis during the Civil War. In 1908, she played an important part in the opening of another home. This was a home for poor and elderly black people. She worked in the home, caring for all the people who lived there. Tubman also turned her attention to women's rights. She was very active in speaking and attending events to support this. She continued to work for the rights of the newly freed black people.

On March 10, 1913, Harriet Tubman died at her home. She was in her early 90s. The U.S. government honored Tubman by giving her a funeral with full military honors. She was buried in Fort Hill Cemetery in Auburn, New York.

Harriet Tubman lived to be more than 90 years old.

Harriet Tubman lived a long and meaningful life. She devoted her life to helping others. Tubman was admired by thousands of black men and women for her courage and for the role she played in freeing slaves. Many others were impressed by her work during the Civil War. Hundreds of people had Harriet Tubman to thank for their freedom, health, and happiness. It is fitting that the inscription on her tombstone reads "Servant of God, Well Done."

Harriet Tubman's gravesite can be visited in Auburn, New York.

1820–1821   Harriet Tubman is born around the year 1820 near Cambridge, Maryland, to Benjamin Ross and Harriet Greene. She is given the name Araminta by her parents and later changes her name to Harriet.

1844   Harriet marries John Tubman.

1849   Tubman receives a note giving her information about the Underground Railroad.

1851–1860   Tubman makes 19 trips to the South on the Underground Railroad.

1859   William and Frances Seward help Tubman purchase a house in Auburn, New York.

1861   The Civil War begins.

1863   Tubman leads a group of black Union soldiers on a victorious raid of a Confederate camp.

1865   The Civil War comes to an end.

1869   Tubman marries Nelson Davis.

1908   The Harriet Tubman Home for the needy and elderly is opened.

1913   Tubman dies on March 10 at home in Auburn, New York. She is buried at Fort Hill Cemetery in Auburn with military honors.

Glossary TERMS

capture (KAP-chur)
To capture means to take someone prisoner by force. A large reward was offered for Harriet Tubman's capture.

courage (KUR-ij)
Courage is bravery in the face of danger. Harriet Tubman showed great courage during her trips on the Underground Railroad.

deeded (DEED-ed)
When property is deeded, ownership of the land is transferred to someone else by sale or gift. Harriet Tubman deeded the property she had purchased in 1896 to the AME Zion Church in 1903.

encountered (en-KOUN-turd)
Something that is met unexpectedly is said to be encountered. Harriet encountered many dangerous situations on the Underground Railroad.

indentured servants (in-DEN-churd SUR-vuhnts)
Indentured servants are people who sign an agreement to work for another person for a specific length of time in exchange for travel expenses, a place to live, and meals. Many men and women from England came to the American colonies to work on plantations as indentured servants.

miserable (MIZ-ur-uh-buhl)
To be miserable means to be very unhappy or uncomfortable. Harriet was miserable away from her parents.

overseer (OV-ur-see-ur)
An overseer is a person who watches over and directs the work of others. An overseer told Harriet to help stop a slave who was attempting to escape.

perils (PER-uhls)
Perils are serious dangers. Tubman and her passengers met many perils on the Underground Railroad.

plantation (plan-TAY-shuhnz)
A plantation is a large farm. Harriet Tubman worked on a plantation.

unconscious (uhn-KON-shuhss)
Someone who is unconscious is not awake or able to feel or think. Harriet was unconscious for a long time after being hit in the head.

Union (YOON-yuhn)
The states that stayed loyal to the U.S. government during the Civil War were referred to as the Union. Harriet Tubman took care of wounded Union army soldiers during the Civil War.

For Further INFORMATION

Web Sites

Visit our homepage for lots of links about Harriet Tubman:
http://www.childsworld.com/links.html

Note to Parents, Teachers, and Librarians:
We routinely verify our Web links to make sure they're safe,
active sites—so encourage your readers to check them out!

Books

Hansen, Joyce, and Gary McGowan. *Freedom Roads: Searching for the Underground Railroad.* Chicago: Cricket Books, 2003.

McDonough, Yona Zeldis, and Nancy Harrison (illustrator). *Who Was Harriet Tubman?* New York: Grosset & Dunlap, 2002.

Sullivan, George. *Harriet Tubman.* New York: Scholastic, 2002.

Troy, Don. *Harriet Ross Tubman.* Chanhassen, Minn.: The Child's World, 1999.

Williams, Carla. *The Underground Railroad.* Chanhassen, Minn.: The Child's World, 2002.

Places to Visit or Contact

The Harriet Tubman Home
To visit the home where Harriet Tubman lived and learn more about her life
180 South Street
Auburn, NY 13201
315/252-2081

National Park Service
To write for information on the National Underground Railroad Network to Freedom program
1849 C Street, N.W.
Washington, DC 20240
202/208-6843

Index

About the Author

CYNTHIA KLINGEL HAS WORKED AS A HIGH SCHOOL English teacher and an elementary school teacher. She is currently the curriculum director for a Minnesota school district. Cynthia Klingel lives with her family in Mankato, Minnesota.

32